Ann Kearns

ANN KEARNS'
SEVENOAKS

The artist and author thank the many people in and around Sevenoaks who have given them so much encouragement and answered their questions so readily.

They also acknowledge their indebtedness to those who have produced earlier books on this lovely town.

ANN KEARNS' SEVENOAKS

RESEARCH & TEXT BY
PATRICK HARPER
1992

Illustrations: Ann Kearns © 1992
Text: Patrick Harper © 1992
Design: Northdown Design Group
Typesetting: Fullpoint
Printing: Able Printing Ltd
ISBN No.: 0 9519946 0 3

FOXPRINT PUBLICATIONS

INTRODUCTION

Sevenoaks in Kent is an ancient town. Like many others, it has suffered or benefitted, depending on your point of view, from the recent activities of property developers. But much of its heart remains.

There are houses, shops and inns dating back through all the centuries to the 14th, many still remarkably true to their time. Look up above the modern shop facias and see the wealth of old brick and tile, wooden beams and sloping Kentish roofs. Peer down narrow passageways to catch a glimpse of an 18th century architrave and some original door furniture.

That is what this book does. It takes you on a gentle stroll through the old town from Oak End and the School in the South along the High Street as far as the Vine. Then it doubles back along the London Road from Bligh's Meadow to the fountain.

As we wander, we discover many facts, and quite a few fictions, about the places we pass. However, it would be wrong to think of this as a history book. It is quite simply a celebration. A celebration of a town that has kept much of its beauty intact if only we take the time to search it out. And a town with many secrets, some of which are revealed in these pages.

We have chosen to ignore Knole apart from a sketch or two. Not that it does not deserve celebrating - far from it. It is just that we have so little room and there is already so much written on this beautiful building.

If Sevenoaks is your home town, we think you will enjoy this sketchbook. If you are not fortunate enough to live here, perhaps these pages will make you want to visit us and see for yourself that there is far more to Sevenoaks than a big house and seven oak trees.

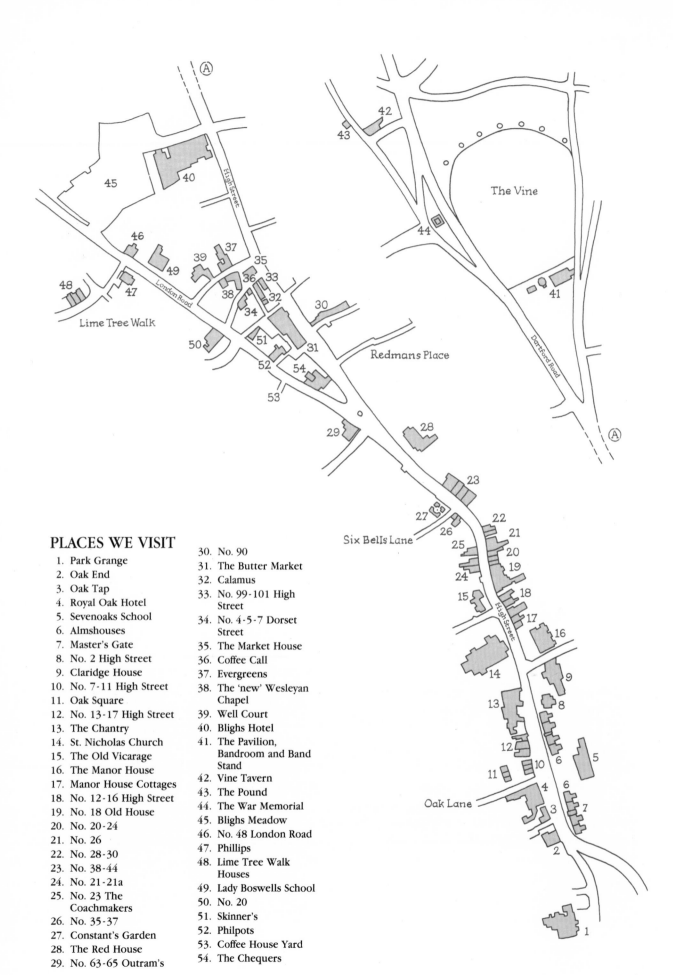

PLACES WE VISIT

1. Park Grange
2. Oak End
3. Oak Tap
4. Royal Oak Hotel
5. Sevenoaks School
6. Almshouses
7. Master's Gate
8. No. 2 High Street
9. Claridge House
10. No. 7-11 High Street
11. Oak Square
12. No. 13-17 High Street
13. The Chantry
14. St. Nicholas Church
15. The Old Vicarage
16. The Manor House
17. Manor House Cottages
18. No. 12-16 High Street
19. No. 18 Old House
20. No. 20-24
21. No. 26
22. No. 28-30
23. No. 38-44
24. No. 21-21a
25. No. 23 The Coachmakers
26. No. 35-37
27. Constant's Garden
28. The Red House
29. No. 63-65 Outram's

30. No. 90
31. The Butter Market
32. Calamus
33. No. 99-101 High Street
34. No. 4-5-7 Dorset Street
35. The Market House
36. Coffee Call
37. Evergreens
38. The 'new' Wesleyan Chapel
39. Well Court
40. Blighs Hotel
41. The Pavilion, Bandroom and Band Stand
42. Vine Tavern
43. The Pound
44. The War Memorial
45. Blighs Meadow
46. No. 48 London Road
47. Phillips
48. Lime Tree Walk Houses
49. Lady Boswells School
50. No. 20
51. Skinner's
52. Philpots
53. Coffee House Yard
54. The Chequers

This book is dedicated to the idea that Sevenoaks is still a beautiful town. Whether its inhabitants regard it as just a place for eating and sleeping while their real world is in London or realise that the town actually possesses all the attributes needed for quite a full life is neither here nor there. We have chosen to ignore activity and concentrate on setting. And there is certainly enough of interest to fill a book. This book.

The oaks near the White Hart

You will find that the graceful yet imposing tower of St. Nicholas keeps a watchful eye over you wherever you walk in upper Sevenoaks. Just note how many times it appears in the pictures in this book.

The bend in the
road to Tonbridge

The old stables ~ Park Grange

L et us start on the south side of town with Park Grange. Once the road to Tonbridge went straight on past Oak End through what is now the gateway to Park Grange. That was before Thomas Lambarde, grandson of the author of England's first county guide (A Perambulation of Kent - published 1576), decided that traffic past his door was too great an inconvenience. He bought a property next door and diverted the road across its land so that Park Grange could be enjoyed in peace.

By the end of the 18th century, the house, an old-fashioned stone mansion as Jane Edwards has it, was sold by Multon Lambarde who was building Beechmont overlooking River Hill. Colonel Austen of Kippington bought the house, demolished the major part and converted the remainder to a farm-house. The present colonial style building was created in 1869/70 and is now a boarding house for girls of Sevenoaks School, having been given to the school by the brothers Johnson.

Park Grange from the south

Park Grange

From the gardens, the girls can look down on what must have been the site of the Battle of Solefields where Jack Cade's Kentish rebels won such an outstanding victory against royalist troops under Sir Humphrey Stafford. This was in 1450 and it is believed that Cade's men followed the defeated enemy as far as the Hogshead (then the Pied Bull) where the final slaughter took place.

Looking towards the site of the Battle of Solefields

Oak End & Little Oak End

Oak End has an interesting history. Like Park Grange, the Oak Tap and the Royal Oak Hotel, it was once part of the Sevenoaks Park Estate. It seems likely that originally a small row of cottages housed gardeners, coachmen etc. to the main house.

In 1843 when a Captain Nepean bought them, they were described as "two messuages or tenements". The captain converted the property in 1858, adding a rear portion whose Georgian-style interior contrasts with the much-timbered front half. So Jane Edwards is right. It is two houses together with the back at the front and front at the back. But it seems that, apart from the cladding, the front may be more genuine than she thought.

Oak End was separated into two some 50 or so years ago by closing off the servant's quarters. The drive beside Little Oak End used to feature a massive turntable for coaches - now buried beneath six inches of tarmacadam.

The present owners of Oak End have repaired the wrought iron lantern bracket that used to hang outside and hope to remount it soon. The design of four clay pipes and tobacco leaves bear out the story that this once adorned the front of a tobacconists' shop at 7 Dorset Street.

The Royal Oak Tap

Why does the Royal Oak Tap have that massive beam over its entrance? Jane Edwards tells us the building was a blacksmith's forge and had been for as long as she could remember. There is some evidence that this was so. She wrote (in 1863) that Mr Guest was the most recent smith and Town Guides show an Edward Guest as a blacksmith in the High Street in 1859. By 1866 it seems his place had been taken by Samuel Read, at least until about 1880. Since 1905 at least, it has been the Oak Tap (sometimes as at present adding 'Royal' though there seems no connection with the Royal Oak Hotel).

The Royal Oak Hotel. This fine stone building was last re-modelled in the mid-19th century having been one of the main coaching inns in the area for many years - originally the 'Bull'. Nearly 200 years ago, coaches arrived here daily with mail for Sevenoaks from the Nag's Head or the Talbot in Southwark.

New owners have built extensively in the grounds behind and appear to have lavished some care on the restoration of the main building.

Oak Lane

Down Oak Lane is an area once known as the Flow Fields because it was so often flooded. This was the main way into Sevenoaks from the Weald of Kent and the top end was only widened some 25 years ago by demolishing No. 5 High Street together with a row of cottages facing Oak Lane itself.

The Royal Oak

School House

SEVENOAKS SCHOOL
AND ALMSHOUSES
FOUNDED 1418
THE PRESENT BUILDINGS WERE
BUILT IN 1724-34 TO THE
DESIGNS OF LORD BURLINGTON

A SEVENOAKS PRESERVATION
SOCIETY PLAQUE

Master's Gate

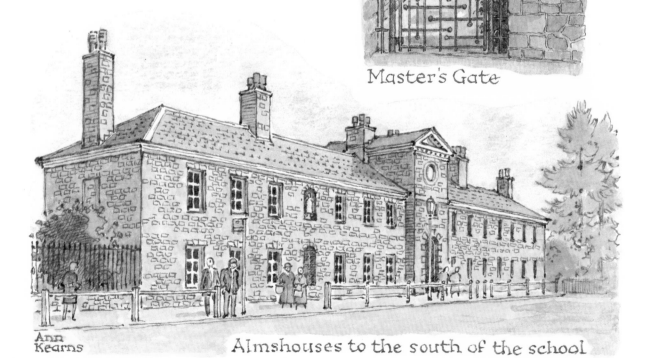

Ann
Kearns

Almshouses to the south of the school

O pposite Oak Lane is the fine main building of the Sevenoaks School flanked by the almshouses all built around 1730. The architect, Richard Boyle, Earl of Burlington, was a disciple of Inigo Jones and the builders used stone from the quarry on Blackhall Farm and sand from Gallows Common.

The school has one of the most ancient foundations in the land dating, it is believed, from 1418 when William Sevenoke established it in a house in the town. It was more firmly rooted when his testament of 1432 endowed it and it is this later date that is usually taken as the true starting point.

In 1560, Queen Elizabeth granted the school the use of her name in letters patent which also provided a new constitution. Elizabethan wood and wattle first gave way to stone in 1631.

Master's Gate. This delightful iron-work structure at the Tonbridge end of the almshouses was made by Tony Wootton, then craftsman-in-residence at Sevenoaks School and erected in 1985 but there has always been a gateway here since the mid 17th century when the Schoolmaster was permitted to go through the hop-garden enclosed by Thomas Lambarde since it gave access to the School House field.

No. 2 High Street, an 18th century house with added bays from the 19th century, has recently been acquired by the school as staff accommodation. It was in this house that Charles Dickens used to lodge on his visits to the town. Two of his daughters are buried in St. Nicholas' churchyard.

No.2 High Street

13

Claridge House

As we shall see, much of the Upper High Street on this east side has now become part of Sevenoaks School.

Claridge House, the school's administration block, was indeed occupied in 1800 by an attorney called J. F. Claridge. Whether or not the house, which dates from a little earlier, was built for his family we do not know. However, following the death of his wife, he found the pressures of coping with his business and four children too great, and shot himself.

The lane next to Claridge House leads to the great house of Knole. As we say in the introduction, so much is known and written about this lovely house that we feel justified in urging the reader to look elsewhere.

Knole Lane

Knole House

Ann Kearns

B ack across the road now to Oak Lane.
7 - 11, an attractive row of late 18th
century houses, hide a secret. Go down
the passage to the right of 11 and you will find . . .

7~11 High Street

Looking to the High Street

. . . another row of three cottages called Oak Square. Of similar date, their original quiet setting has been pleasantly disturbed by tennis courts for the school.

From the square you catch another glimpse of St. Nicholas' tower.

Oak Square

No 13 The Old Post Office

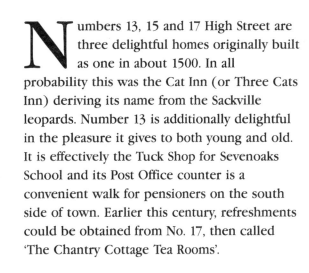

Numbers 13, 15 and 17 High Street are three delightful homes originally built as one in about 1500. In all probability this was the Cat Inn (or Three Cats Inn) deriving its name from the Sackville leopards. Number 13 is additionally delightful in the pleasure it gives to both young and old. It is effectively the Tuck Shop for Sevenoaks School and its Post Office counter is a convenient walk for pensioners on the south side of town. Earlier this century, refreshments could be obtained from No. 17, then called 'The Chantry Cottage Tea Rooms'.

No.17 once The Chantry Cottage Tea Rooms

Ann Kearns

Next door, the Chantry sits impressively on the site of the house built in the 13th century for Henry de Gand (or Gandave - "of Ghent") the rector of Sevenoaks to whom a grant of chantry was made in 1257 by Boniface, Archbishop of Canterbury. The chantry itself would have been a side chapel in St. Nicholas Church dedicated to the souls of the father and mother of Henry de Gand. A priest would have been appointed to say special prayers and, over the years, the income from his endowment would have been sufficient to enable a sizeable house to be built for him.

The chantry was abolished in 1548 and the land and house sold. This present house dates from 1686, with its extension (Chantry House and stable block) from 1905. The blind 'windows' of the main house are architectural features owing nothing to the window tax. The

St Nicholas over the roof tops

Chantry House

The Chantry

rooms within are well lit by other true windows. The rear of the brick building is in attractive Kentish Ragstone. The cellars include what appears to be the remains of the earlier ecclesiastical building. It is from this time, incidentally, that St. Nicholas had both a rector and, to assist him, a vicar. The duties were merged in the late 18th century.

Intricate gates of The Chantry

One of the
peal of
eight bells

There is mention
of a church on
this site in 'The
Textus Roffensis'
in AD 1122,
known then as
Seouenaca.

St Nicholas Church Sevenoaks

Ann Kearns

Footpath through the churchyard

hat can we say about St. Nicholas, the parish church of Sevenoaks? Please go and see this fine building either to worship or admire. Go round the back, too, for a very different view and chance to walk through two wonderfully peaceful old churchyards. The names of famous Sevenoaks' families are recorded on stone memorials which stand, some askew, in a delightful wilderness.

The south porch

The west side of the tower

The 'new' graveyard

P resumably the Old Vicarage ceased to have any religious use after the merging of duties referred to. Certainly it has been a private residence now for some two hundred years. Like many old places, there is a legend of a ghost - the little grey lady. But it seems to have been laid to rest. She has certainly not put in an appearance in the last quarter century and it seems she was associated with the early 19th century extension that once ran in front and down the side of this building. Removed after the last war, she seems to have gone with the rubble. Try to see the house in the late Spring when wisteria hangs in huge bunches on the railings on either side of the front or in the Autumn when the pleasant early 18th century features of the house itself glow with crimson creeper.

The Old Vicarage
from Rectory Lane

The Old Vicarage

Manor House

Before we get too far down the road, let us return to the Manor House on the other side. Now part of the school, it dates from the late 18th century. According to Jane Edwards, it was built by the Duke of Dorset for a certain Captain Coast who had

No 8 & 10
Manor House Cottages

lost a great deal of his property by gaming with the Duke. It reputedly served as the Dower House to Knole and stands on the site of one of our oldest inns - the New Inn - which is recorded back to the 15th Century.

Manor House Cottages (8 & 10) are pleasant 18th century buildings originally part of the stables for the Manor House but now staff quarters for the school.

No.12 High Street

Schoolgirls now enjoy the splendours of the next row of houses. Numbers 12 to 16 are from the nineteenth century. Towards the end of that century, No. 12 was occupied by a baker and corn dealer. In the 1880's it was run by E. Martin and at the turn of the century by F. H. Brigden. Mr Brigden obviously prospered and moved to bigger premises in London Road.

In the 1920s, No. 12 was divided into two with 12a occupied by the Lurcook family and 12 by Mr Beck, a local gardener.

No. 14 was certainly a private dwelling (of Mrs Marchant) for much of the first half of this century.

There was a pump down the yard, still operative in the 20s though the houses by then had running water.

No 14 High Street

Old House

The lovely Old House (No. 18) was built around 1700. Jane Edwards (and others following on) suggests that it was once an inn but this is most unlikely. Its architecture is that of a superior domestic dwelling, a fine town house for fine people. The Austen family lived here for many years and, more recently, it had been the home of the Constants referred to later in the section on Six Bells Lane.

20-24, also from around 1700 but much altered, provide school staff accommodation.

It is good that much of the sensitive group of Upper High Street properties are now owned by the school which can surely be entrusted with their careful maintenance.

No's 20~24 High Street

From a painting of 1840

From a late 19th Century view.

N o. 26 High Street, which currently houses a music shop and a property agency in the 19th century front extensions, would look much like the Old Vicarage if those extensions were removed, though it is thought that the house dates from the late 1700s. During the first half of this century, a succession of ladies ran an "art needlework repository" here and Eve Strutt remembers Madame Stephanie who used to trim hats.

The Old Coffee House is probably 17th century in origin with elevations added a century later. In the early 1900s, George Budgen, grocer, occupied No. 28 and Edward Richter, tobacconist, No. 30. By 1917, the Budgens owned both shops (grocer and upholsterer). Bert was still there to the end of the 50s.

Our pictures show how little 26 to 30 have changed since 1840 apart from the two front extensions to 26, whose old door still exists.

The same view today

The original doorway of No.26

26

No's 38~44 High Street

Park House

when Park Grange became the main girl's boarding house in 1987/8, it was decided to name No. 38 as Park House - only to discover later that this was, indeed, the original 18th century name.

No 44 High Street

Numbers 38-44 High Street are a pleasant row of listed 18th century houses, though 44 has a modern "Georgian-style" front added. No. 38 houses staff for the girls boarding at the school, and

Kingsley House

The Coachmakers

Kingsley House (now Nos. 21 & 21a). Some 60 years ago, this housed a school run by Miss Downing and her helper Miss Seymour - a formidable pair. Mrs Strutt remembers her brother asking Miss Seymour "why is a monkey like a mole?" and supplying the answer "because his tail's above his hole". He was severely caned, of course. As was Eve herself when, aged about 10, she cycled down the rockery for a dare, scattering the plants as she went. There were only around 8 children at the school so the culprit was soon persuaded to confess.

It is recorded that Mr Pett, the first of the famous family of cricket bat makers, lived and worked in a cottage behind No. 21 around 1745. Possibly this was the Old House Cottage which is certainly old enough to qualify.

23 High Street. Originally a private house, this had become the Coachmaker's Arms by the early 19th century and remained so until the 1960's when it became a house again. There is no trace of a coachmakers hereabouts though one possibly existed at the back of the Royal Oak or down the yard opposite Rayley's Corner (35, 37 High Street).

Take a stroll down Six Bells Lane and look back towards the High Street at the wonderful array of roofs. Originally the Six Bells Inn was at the corner, the name for pub and lane coming from the six bells of the St. Nicholas' peal. The Reverend Thomas Curteis DD rector from 1747 to 1775 caused the six bells to be melted down and added enough new metal to make the fine eight bell peal of today.

There has been a deal of 'prettying-up' of the properties down the lane. Not that this is a bad thing. Certainly it is greatly to be preferred to the demolition that has occurred elsewhere in this old part of town.

Towards Six Bells Lane

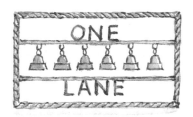

Attractive house-sign at No.1 Six Bells Lane

Looking down the lane.

The 'cat-slide' roof behind the High Street

Ann Kearns

29

The garden in memory
of Mr and Mrs Constant

This is the pretty little garden given to the town in 1949 by the children of Mr & Mrs Constant in memory of their parents who had lived in the Old House and owned much of the property nearby. A delightful thought and a peaceful spot especially for the older residents.

Incidentally, the well for the houses in Six Bells Lane was in the grounds of the Old Rectory at the foot of the hill so that, unlike Jack and Jill, people had to struggle up the hill with their pails full of water.

Another view of St Nicholas

Looking up Six Bells Lane

The Red House

T he Red House was built in 1686 for Thomas Couchman of Tooting and occupied between 1688 and his death in 1734 by the redoubtable Dr Fuller - a physician who personally tested all his remedies before offering them to his patients and was the scourge of those who abused public office. Greatly admired by the rich and loved by the poor whose cause he championed over mismanagement of the charity controlling the School and Almshouses.

By 1734 the house was owned by Francis Austen a local solicitor whose famous niece Jane visited him here in 1788 at the age of 12.

The Red House & former entrance to stables

Outram's

Certainly one of the most strikingly beautiful buildings in the town is Outram's shop at 63 and 65 High Street. The facing of fish-scale tiles dates from the 19th century but the house they cover (for it was once a house) was built around the 15th century as the residence of the reeve or agent of the Archbishop of Canterbury. A fine old stone fireplace can still be seen bearing the arms of Archbishops Chichele (1414-43) and Warham (1502-32). It certainly remained a house for many years but by the mid 19th century W. Loveland had a leather buiness there. On his death, around 1870, his assistant James Outram took over the business which prospered under his guidance.

Now let us fork right at the fountain, erected in 1882 but no longer providing water for horses or the beasts brought to market.

From a painting of The Shambles 1840

The Old Market Place. It seems likely that the town market in mediaeval times took in all of the triangle of land from the fountain down High Street and London Road to Bank Street. In the early 13th century there were no buildings on the site but over the years wealthy traders began to put up more permanent shops.

We will pass by the 16th century Chequers (reluctantly) but return to it at the end of the book.

The Fountain

On the other side of the road Redman's Place was once what writers in the last century referred to as "a stew". A narrow alleyway with some 16 cottages, it was remembered by Mrs Elsie Wright as "Clothes-prop Alley" because many of the cottages having no back yards, "they always had their washing out front - dustbins too."

In earlier times, the alley led to the first Methodist Chapel built in Sevenoaks and opened by John Wesley himself in 1774. It was later abandoned for the 'new' chapel in Bank Street (now shops and a restaurant).

The construction of Barclays Bank a few years ago removed the last traces of Clothes-prop Alley - one demolition not to be regretted.

hinges were bought one at a time and nails by the pound instead of today's packages that always contain three too many or one too few. The present name of "Mousetrap", however, refers to the long-running play and not to ironmongery.

Webb's Alley

No. 90 High Street

90 High Street is a delightful late 18th century building clad in timber partly marked out in ashlar style. It is remembered by many as Franks the ironmongers where screws and

The Butter Market

Back again to the small area of the Saturday market. The Butter Market was at the corner of the two passageways - one to London Road the other to the Shambles - by the Lloyds Bank building. Here on fair days (July 10 and October 12) were held Hiring Fairs for servants.

Perhaps the oldest building in the area is that in the Shambles currently owned by Calamus. The first crown-post roof in the town, it dates from 1450 to 1530. The two old properties in High Street, 99 and 101, were originally detached and separated by around 5ft at ground level and only 2ft at first floor. 99 is the older (about 1575) while 101 was built some 25 years later. The date of 1603 on 7 Dorset Street seems to be accurate, with 4/5 (Sevenoaks Travel) roughly the same age. The coffee shop (still thought of as Buckwells) dates from the same period though the front was added later. The Woolwich Building Society occupies the Old Market House built in 1843 to replace an Elizabethan structure on stilts. Assizes had been held here and Jane Edwards tells a harrowing tale of the trial in 1554 of Sir William Isly and a Mr Mantel of Wrotham for insurrection. Local feelings ran

high and once the pair was found guilty they were speedily taken to execution on Gallows Common (roughly where Bradbourne Road and Camden Road are today).

The Shambles

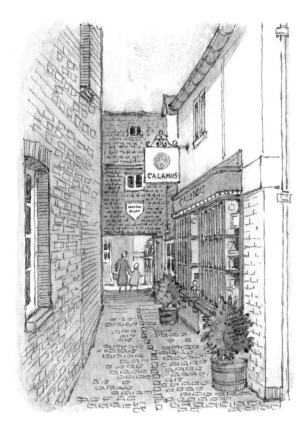

Calamus in the ancient
Shambles area of Sevenoaks

The first crown post roof in
Sevenoaks dating from about
1450 ~ 1530

Ann Kearns

Dorset Street entrance
to The Shambles beside
a former grocer's store
established in Nelson's
time, known as

Buckwell

No 8 Dorset Street ~ the coffee shop

35

The head of James the First in stone is embedded in the wall of No. 7 Dorset Street.

No 7 Dorset Street ~ Sevenoaks once a tobacconist's shop

The Old Market House (from an old drawing) built before 1554. Replaced by the present Regency building.

Ann Kearns

Dorset Street ~ looking from London Road.

No's 99 & 101 High Street and Market House built in 1843

The 'new' Chapel
Bank Street

On page 33 we mentioned the building of this new Wesleyan chapel, now a restaurant and group of shops. Evergreens. Until very recently, this old pub was called the Black Boy and had a liveried black servant as its sign. The name, however, came from the Blackboy family who owned land here-abouts in Tudor times. Bank Street on which it stands was Black Boy Lane until early this century when, it is said, it was changed to celebrate Young's Bank. This had operated in the early 19th century from premises round the corner in London Road. The inn's present building dates from the late 1700s.

The garden and orchard behind the Black Boy in older times joined onto the gardens of Bethlehem Farm (Bligh's Hotel is on the site of the farmhouse). The trees still standing in Blighs Meadow represent the northern boundary of the Blackboy land.

Evergreens

Bank Street

Well Court

H ere is an imaginative development from the 1960s. Well Court was created using some existing buildings and shows a proper regard for its surroundings.

Looking towards Bank Street

The well ~ Well Court

Blighs Hotel   about 1900

C ontinuing along High Street, we reach Blighs Hotel, originally the farmhouse for the 'Farm on the Vine', later 'Bethlehem Farm' and then Bligh's Farm' after its new owner. A brewery, Bligh's Brewery, was established on land facing the side of the hotel where Dorothy Perkins shop now stands.

The front elevation remains much as it was up to the early part of this century but all else has been much remodelled.

Samuel Bligh had run the Royal Crown Hotel (roughly where Russell & Bromley is today) so we are not surprised to read in Harrod's Postal

Bethlehem Farm in 1800
(from an old drawing)

& Commercial Directory for 1867 that, following the family acquisition of Bethlehem Farm, he now ran a "private family hotel replete with comfort and accommodation, charges moderate, pleasure gardens, etc." John Bligh's adjacent brewery was at this time referred to as the Holmesdale Brewery.

There has long been a legend that Bethlehem Farm was owned by, or at least associated with, the "Bedlam" Hospital in London and that its inmates were sent for restful treatment to the country town of Sevenoaks. The archivist at Bethlehem Royal Hospital states categorically that there has never been any connection between the hospital and any property in Sevenoaks. She blames Jane Edwards for having started off a story that simply refuses to die.

Bligh's Hotel about 1900

A view from one of the prettiest cricket grounds in Kent

Sometimes it seems as though Sevenoaks and cricket are synonymous. After all, the Vine is not only one of the prettiest grounds in the land it is also one of the oldest. It was here in 1734 that a match took place that was the first ever to be reported in the national press. And it seems that cricket had been played on the Vine for many years before that.

The Pound

There are more views of the Vine on pages 42 and 43.

Some of the stately houses on Park Lane were built in time for their occupants to enjoy a fine view of that famous game. Much of the property on Pound Lane that faces the ground comes from the nineteenth century. But it seems likely, knowing cricketers, that there has been a Vine Tavern hereabouts for as long as there has been a cricket ground.

Talking of Pound Lane, the old town pound still exists behind its wooden rail fence, though the electricity people seem to have taken over a part of it.

Sevenoaks has other strong connections with cricket. The school has produced some good players over the years and at least one member of the Pett family still produced memorable cricket bats from his workshops in the High Street in the 19th century.

In the mid 19th century, Jonathan Morgan made cricket balls and Henry Sutton cricket bats and wickets. Both lived nearby on St. Johns Hill.

Of course, until the latter half of the 19th century, the Vine and its houses effectively stood outside the town. So there is little of great interest to take our eye on our return walk to Blighs.

The War Memorial

However, the War Memorial deserves mention. This fine memorial was unveiled on Sunday October 24th 1920 to commemorate the 225 men from Sevenoaks who died in the war - about one in six of those who answered the call. The sculptor, C. A. Walker, produced not only a fine model of a British Tommy as the main feature, but also two side panels showing, in relief, ship's gunners on one side and RFC crew and airplane on the other. Like many throughout the land, it now commemorates the local dead of World War II and is the town's focal point each year on Remembrance Sunday.

Turning along the side of Blighs, the area known as Blighs Meadow offers a bleak prospect. A car park, and a somewhat desolate one at that. There are plans afoot for development but little agreement between the Council and the public as to the form it should take.

These trees mark the original boundary between Blighs Farm and the Blackboy estate.

The original boundary of Bligh's Farm

Ann
Kearns

In 1987 a storm felled
six of the seven old
oaks. Seven new trees
were planted in 1988.

The Vine oaks known
as the 'Coronation Trees'
were planted in 1902
to commemorate the
coronation of Edward VII

The Vine with its
distant views of
the North Downs.

42

The Vine ground was given to the town by the
3rd Duke of Dorset ~ himself a keen patron
of cricket ~ in 1773

weathervane on
the new pavilion

the bandroom & bandstand

The Vine Tavern

Ann
Kearns

Round the corner, this doorway with its beautiful lights, together with the timber ashlar-style front, must have been the reasons for making No. 48 London Road a listed 18th century building.

This delightful stone building (now occupied by Phillips the auctioneers) was first built as a Savings Bank in the early 19th century. A suitably solid and four-square

No. 48 London Road

Phillips ~ 49 London Road

Back on London Road, the Lady Boswell School building went up in 1818 as a result of co-operation between the architect who had restored St. Nicholas church (S. P. Cookerell) and local builder Henry Rose. The ragstone came from the now disused quarry just inside the hole in the wall in Seal Hollow Road.

LIME TREE WALK

building, it invites you to walk along Lime Tree Walk beside it and enter a very different world. Once the Lime Tree Hotel was the leading temperance hotel in the area and a mecca for turn-of-the-century cyclists. The hotel may have gone but the row of attractive houses, designed and built by Sir Thomas Jackson, remains. They were intended as a housing experiment for working class people in a high class residential area in 1878.

Lime Tree Walk

Lady Boswells School

L ady Boswell gave the school its endowment in 1675 and, until this new school was built, the scholars had either been taught at private homes or as extra pupils in established schools such as Sevenoaks School.

Philpots

Just look at the lovely sweep of weather-boarding on the first floor side view of Philpots.

Skinner's butchers shop at 20 London Road is a fine example of the continuing use of an early 18th century building that must, from its position, have been "in trade" since the beginning. A photograph taken 130 years ago shows it as a butcher's shop even then, and looking very much the same as today.

In 1986/7, when 21, 23 and 25 London Road were being transformed from the old W. H. Smith shop to Paydens the chemists, local historians were given a rare opportunity for a full examination of one of our oldest buildings. It seems that No. 21 (the left-hand end when viewing the shop from the road) is the oldest part dating from around 1500-1530. It has a crown post from this period and smoke-blackened roof timbers from the open fire that would have been on the ground floor. The extreme left wall contains a blocked-off inglenook from about 1596 telling us that a chimney was first introduced at that time. Numbers 23 and 25 were built between 1670 and 1700. The north wall by the surgery is clearly 17th century and the brickwork seems to have remained untouched since it was built.

Skinner's

Coffee House Yard

Coffee House Yard - in here used to be the Granary in which John Wesley preached a few time before the first meeting house was built (see Redman's Place). Our view from here reveals something of the more sinister side of the Chequers Inn. Reputedly, there has been an inn here since the 1100's. The main part of the existing inn dates from the 16th or early 17th century and succeeding centuries have made their additions - as is usual in a much used, and much loved, building. The Chequers name seems to have been used as far back as 1707.

But back to the sinister side. In a small enclosed area between the inn and the back of No. 4 London Road stood a gallows. Sometimes it was convenient to hold local sessions and Manor Courts at the inn. Executions were then carried out on the gallows and the bodies buried in the adjoining lime-pit. This piece of land remains Crown property even today.

The London Road side of The Chequers

Not surprisingly, such a past gives rise to legend. It is said that a non-alcoholic spirit is to be experienced in the Chequers. A lady who, from an upstairs window saw her son hanged, herself expired on the spot. Her anguished shade at times walks the upstairs rooms. They say the window was bricked up to prevent any recurrence.

The attractive design of the inn sign here dates back to the siege of Calais in 1348. It is derived from the arms of the Earls of Warrenne and Surrey who bore this device into battle. Subsequently, Edward IV granted them the privelege of licensing ale-houses. This seemed reason enough to adopt this design during major repairs and restoration in 1949.

There is more, much more, to find in Sevenoaks. While we do not have any more room, we hope we have whetted your appetite to do a little gentle exploring of your own.

47

SOURCES

Information for this book has come from many sources. The principal printed ones are:

Dr Gordon Ward
Sevenoaks Essays

Sir John Dunlop
The Pleasant Town of Sevenoaks

Frank Richards
Old Sevenoaks

Gordon Anckorn
A Sevenoaks Camera
Sevenoaks Memories

Jane Edwards
Her Recollections (sometimes unreliable)

Sevenoaks & District Guide and Handbook

Bagshaw, Post Office, Harrod's Postal and Kelly's Directories for Kent for 19th century.

Archive material located in the Sevenoaks Reference Library including valuable work done by the Sevenoaks District Architectural History Group.

Among personal recollections used are those of:

Eve Strutt (nee Humphrey) who once lived at the corner of Six Bells Lane.

Elsie Wright (born 1908 in Ide Hill) who remembers that walking into Sevenoaks from Ide Hill "took about an hour".

THE END